c. 1905

Greetings from Colorado

by Marshall Sprague

GRAPHIC ARTS CENTER PUBLISHING COMPANY, PORTLAND, OREGON

c. 1916

International Standard Book Number 0-932575-72-2
Library of Congress Catalog Number 88-80538
Copyright © MCMLXXXVIII by Graphic Arts Center Publishing Company
P.O. Box 10306, Portland, Oregon 97210 • 503/226-2402
Editor-in-Chief • Douglas A. Pfeiffer
Associate Editor • Jean Andrews
Illustrations Assistant • Alison M. Morba
Designer • Robert Reynolds
Typographer • Harrison Typesetting, Inc.
Color Separations • Trade Litho
Printer • Dynagraphics
Binder • Lincoln & Allen

Printed in the United States of America

A special debt of gratitude is owed to the deltiologists whose extraordinary postcard collections and enduring affection for Colorado have made this book possible: Hazel Graves, Ed Bailey, Betty Watchous, Foxy E. L. Hawpe, Carl Kallgren, Marian and Peter Maronn.

c. 1910

Contents

Circa dates refer to a ten-year time period largely determined by the printing styles of a particular era, the subject matter depicted, and other information providing clues to the date of publication.

Arapahoe Peaks, Colo.

Preface

BY CONGRESSWOMAN PATRICIA SCHROEDER

Explorers returning to the East from Colorado told tales as tall as mountains and as vivid as thundering buffaloes. The artists who accompanied those early expeditions not only illuminated the tales but also, by graphically illustrating and embellishing them, revealed them to be true.

By the turn-of-the-century, postcards could be bought off the rack and dispatched to envious neighbors and relatives back home. "Having a great time. Wish you were here!" would be scribbled on one side of the card, while a picture of the Garden of the Gods or Pikes Peak tantalized on the flipside.

If rain pelted the tent in Rocky Mountain National Park, if the car broke down half-way between Telluride and Pueblo, if the kids scowled and yelped for days on end—no matter. The postcard enshrined the visit in the imagination.

GREETINGS FROM COLORADO is a book of enshrined vacation memories, a snapshot history of the state, from 1900 through the 1950s: Miners inside a Cripple Creek tunnel; a wedding atop Pikes Peak; two skiers on Aspen Mountain; the interior of the Nanking American and Chinese Restaurant and the exterior of the Arapahoe Butter Shop; Silver Plume's main street with its view of Black Hawk; and mountain lakes and peaks galore.

GREETINGS FROM COLORADO is a 316-postcard salute to the natural marvels and the marvelous people of the Rocky Mountain State.

13608 THE LURE OF THE TRAIL.

c. 1920

c. 1910

c. 1910

c. 1940

c. 1910

A guardian of the wilderness and a promoter of women's rights, the ninety-year-old Colorado Mountain Club counts among its members the first Colorado woman in the United States House of Representatives, Patricia Schroeder.

Introduction

Historians tell us that the first postcards in the United States appeared in the 1890s to promote the World's Columbian Exposition in Chicago. Then came the "Golden Age of Postcards" from 1907 to 1915, when millions of cards were mailed in the United States and worldwide.

Those early postcards were lovingly created by proud communities to show the beauty, romance, or excitement of their landscape. If the cards exaggerated and presented a dream world, visitors did not mind because it appeared a wonder world anyway.

The broad appeal of the cards was due partly to their low cost—a nickel or a dime apiece—and to the penny postage. Visitors to Colorado sent them to friends back home to show them where they had been—places such as Rocky Mountain National Park, the Garden of the Gods, or the steam cog train up Pikes Peak.

Becoming more specialized as their numbers have increased, collectors determine the price of a card by its age, availability, condition, and public interest in the subject.

Restored by modern printing techniques to their original luster, the postcards in this book date from the "Gay Nineties" to World War II and are organized geographically. The text gives a brief overview of the state's history during that period.

These postcards may be relics of yesterday, but by showing us the world as it once appeared, they give us a unique feeling for the sweep of history.

c. 1940

West Spanish Peaks and Dyke, Altitude 13, 720 feet Huerfano Co. Colo.

c. 1910

9340. The Collegiate Peaks, Yale, Harvard and Princeton, Colo.

c. 1910

3010. Mount of the Holy Cross, Colo.

c. 1910

8695. Arapahoe Peaks, Colorado

c. 1910

The Colorado Rockies

The first American to explore Colorado was a twenty-seven-year-old Indian fighter from New Jersey, Captain Zebulon Montgomery Pike. With his party of sixteen, Pike rode up the Arkansas River to examine the unknown territory—purchased by Thomas Jefferson from Napoleon in 1803—between St. Louis and the Continental Divide.

On November 15, 1806, the Pike party topped a ridge on Colorado's Eastern Slope near the present town of Las Animas. Far ahead, they could see under the bluest of skies a shining eminence, later named Pikes Peak (altitude 14,110 feet).

They reached the Front Range of the Rockies at Pueblo, but failed to climb Pikes Peak because of deep snow and sub-zero weather. Instead, the hardy explorers spent their Christmas near the present town of Salida in thirty-below weather, huddled around pine fires and sheltered by soaring uplands that include the state's highest peak, Mount Elbert (14,431 feet), and the beautiful Collegiate Range (Mounts Harvard, Yale, and Princeton).

Next, Pike led his men down Wet Mountain Valley and over the Sangre de Cristo Range to the spacious San Luis Valley. There, near the present town of Alamosa, they found the Rio Grande River and that eerie tourist attraction, the Great Sand Dunes National Monument, which lies below magnificent Blanca Peak. Zebulon Pike went on to other exploits, but before Pikes Peak was named in his honor, he was killed during the War of 1812.

In 1820, Major Long followed Pike's example of fearless exploration by traveling up the Platte River to the future site of Denver,

c. 1915

1589. A Mountain Home.

c. 1910

where he discovered Long's Peak above Estes Park. His botanist, Edwin James, climbed Pikes Peak by what is now the Barr Trail above Manitou, used today by thousands of hikers.

During the 1860s, most of the state's fifty-three mountains over fourteen thousand feet were conquered by frantic gold seekers prospecting for riches along the Continental Divide. Then the expert climbers of Hayden's Geological Survey of 1873 scaled Uncompahgre Peak above Lake City, Sneffels Peak near Telluride, and the lovely San Juan Mountains between Ouray and Durango. Their maps showed that most of the great rivers of the West—the Colorado, the Rio Grande, and both of the Platte rivers—began in the Colorado Rockies.

But the Rockies were still unknown to the general public. Then in 1909, a Colorado Springs resident, Spencer Penrose, helped create the Colorado State Highway Department to improve highway conditions. In 1915, Penrose spent $250,000 of his own money to build a highway to the top of Pikes Peak. To publicize it, Penrose staged the Pikes Peak Hill Climb, which showed that the improved cars of 1916 could go anywhere. With that established, Penrose believed that soon everybody would travel in the Rockies by car instead of by train.

Today, Coloradans argue endlessly about their favorite Colorado highway. In summer, some opt for the Trail Ridge Road (U.S. 34) from Estes Park across Rocky Mountain National Park. Another popular road, the "Million Dollar Highway," runs from Ouray for seventy-three miles through Silverton to Durango past the beautiful Mount Sneffels and the Needles and Grenadier ranges. Another memorable trip starts at Walsenburg on United States 160 and goes over La Veta Pass to the San Luis Valley and the Great Sand Dunes National Monument, then on to Wolf Creek Pass, one of Colorado's loveliest Divide crossings.

8226. Pike's Peak, from Woodland Park, on Colo. Midland Ry.

c. 1910

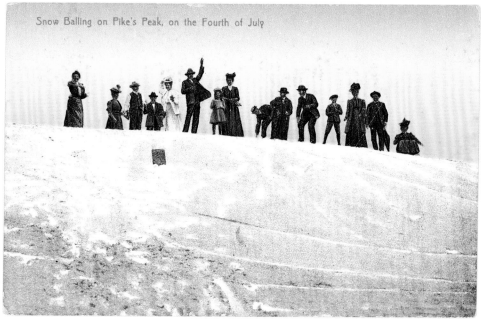

Snow Balling on Pike's Peak, on the Fourth of July

c. 1910

FIRST WEDDING ON THE HIGHEST TOWER IN THE WORLD, SOLEMNIZED BY J. WESLEY NEELY, JULY 19, 1905. SUMMIT PIKE'S PEAK, ALTITUDE 14,109 FEET

COPYRIGHT BY J.W.NEELY, 1909.

c. 1909

Since 1890, tourists have been thrilled by the nine-mile trip by cog railway up Pikes Peak. The old steam-powered trains have been replaced by diesel engines, which continue taking cars up the steep grade from April through October.

c. 1910

c. 1930

c. 1910

Built after getting a federal permit from Teddy Roosevelt, David Moffat's railroad between Denver and Craig through Gore Canyon, one of hundreds of deep canyons cut by rains as the Rockies rose from ancient seas.

1551. Fraser Canon, Colorado.

c. 1910

1685 Echo Cliffs, Grand Canon, Colorado.

c. 1910

ON THE DENVER & RIO GRANDE WESTERN RAILROAD — THRU THE ROCKIES, NOT AROUND THEM

GLENWOOD CANON OF THE COLORADO RIVER. ROYAL GORGE AND MOFFAT TUNNEL ROUTES

7A-H859

c. 1925

613. View of Dyke, Valley and Town from the Red Rocks.
Park of the Red Rocks and Garden of the Titans, Mt. Morrison, Colo.

c. 1908

8922. Lilly Lake, Colo.

Trout Lake, in the Silver San Juan, Colo.

c. 1910

c. 1910

1812   Beautiful Glacier Lake, Colorado.
C. & N. W. R. R. *"Switzerland Trail of America."*

N114:—ST. MARY'S GLACIER, COLORADO

c. 1940

c. 1910

7415 Chipeta Falls, Black Canon, Colo.

c. 1910

6716. BRIDAL VEIL FALLS, COLORADO

c. 1906

15125. Seven Falls, South Cheyenne
Canon, Colorado Springs
Colorado.

c. 1915

The Pikes Peak watershed supplies Colorado Springs and produces these waterfalls. The stairway at the tourist attraction of Seven Falls leads to the original grave of Helen Hunt Jackson. The grave is now at Evergreen Cemetery.

c. 1930

c. 1930

c. 1930

Since 1917, ski jumping has been an annual event in Steamboat Springs. But the real ski boom began in the 1930s, when skiers discovered Winter Park and Berthoud Pass, often trying to travel before roads were cleared.

SKIING BORTHOUD PASS

c. 1930

SKI-ING THRU THE SOFT SNOW ON ASPEN MT. , ASPEN, COLO.

Sanborn W·3239

c. 1950

In the early days, Colorado skiers had to herringbone laboriously up the steep slopes. Then came the first primitive rope tows – dangerous and totally unreliable – powered by Model-T Ford engines. Finally, in January 1947, Aspen discarded its clumsy tow when Walter Paepcke built a three-mile-long chair lift on Ajax Mountain for $250,000.

c. 1925

c. 1925

In the 1920s, motorists drove up the new Fall River Road and across Rocky Mountain National Park to the Continental Divide at Milner Pass. Now used by millions of motorists from May through early November, this road, later renamed the Trail Ridge Highway, reaches a height of 12,183 feet—the highest point on any federal highway.

15760. June 25th—Fall River Road. Rocky Mountain National Park

c. 1925

329 TIMBERLINE TREES OF THE ROCKIES

OUTPOSTS OF THE FORESTS DEFYING THE WINTRY STORMS OF THE HIGH PLACES   113330

c. 1920

249. Snow Cuts on the Divide.

c. 1905

The Rocky Mountain Hunter's Winter Quarters

c. 1910

13705 SNOW PLOW, MARSHALL PASS, COLO.

c. 1920

c. 1920

c. 1940

Although it boasts many reservoirs and rivers, Colorado has only one genuine lake-side resort: Grand Lake, on Middle Park at the west end of Trail Ridge Road. Large enough for sailing, the lake hosts yacht races each August.

c. 1940

7487. Stanley Hotel, Estes Park, Colo.

c. 1915

15707. Gem Lake and Longs Peak, Estes Park, Colorado, Rocky Mountain National Park

c. 1945

ROCKY MOUNTAIN NATIONAL—ESTES PARK, COLORADO, A SUMMER PARADISE FOR THE KIDDIES.
Burlington Route—Direct to the Park.

c. 1920

15772. Longs Peak from Porch of Stanley Hotel, Estes Park, Colo. Rocky Mountain National Park

c. 1945

8891. Mt. Fairchild from Estes Park, Colo.

15445. Gateway to Denver Mountain Parks

c. 1920

15650. Echo Lake, Colorado, Denver Mountain Parks

c. 1920

349—Tinytown—The Toy Village in Turkey Creek Cañon

Denver Mountain Parks, Colorado

5655-29-N

c. 1945

16036. Shelter House, Denver Mountain Parks, Colorado
On Victory Highway

c. 1920

c. 1910

15666. Buffalo Bill Museum and Grave, Lookout Mt., Colo.

c. 1930

Buffalo Bill and Sitting Bull

© MRS. JOHNNY BAKER

Buffalo Bill Memorial Museum, Lookout Mountain, Colorado

c. 1940

Buffalo Bill Cody, Denver's beloved showman, brought the Grand Duke Alexis, son of Russia's Czar Alexander II, to Denver in 1873. In his honor, ten thousand residents attended one of the most elaborate balls ever held in Denver.

Art Gallery, Buffalo Bill Memorial Museum, Lookout Mountain, Colorado

© MRS. JOHNNY BAKER

c. 1930

CLEAR CREEK FROM COLORAW POINT, LOOKOUT MOUNTAIN, COLO.

c. 1925

AEROPLANE VIEW OF LARIAT TRAIL TO LOOKOUT MOUNTAIN, COLORADO

c. 1925

355   LOST (LINCOLN) LAKE FROM THE MT. EVANS HIGHWAY

DENVER MOUNTAIN PARKS, COLO.

c. 1925

BURRO RIDING IS GREAT IN COLORADO

c. 1910

Creation Rock, Mount Morrison, Colorado.

c. 1910

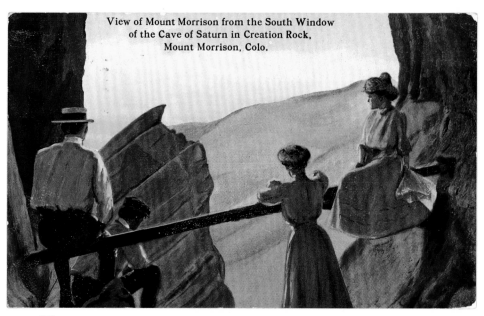

View of Mount Morrison from the South Window of the Cave of Saturn in Creation Rock, Mount Morrison, Colo.

c. 1910

N178 AMPHITHEATRE, RED ROCKS PARK, COLORADO

c. 1940

On the Seat of Pluto, Park of the Red Rocks, Mt. Morrison, Colo.

c. 1910

SINKING TITANIC. PARK OF THE RED ROCKS. DENVER MOUNTAIN PARKS. MORRISON. COLO

c. 1915

TUNNEL, CREATION ROCK DRIVE, PARK OF THE RED ROCKS, DENVER MOUNTAIN PARKS, COLORADO

c. 1940

15791. The Pueblo Park of the Red Rocks, Denver Mt. Parks, Colorado

c. 1915

Initiated in 1912 by Mayor Speer, Denver's Red Rocks Park was enlarged in 1941 to 639 acres by Mayor Ben Stapleton. Inspired by amphitheatres in Sicily, park director George Cranmer instructed architect Burnam Hoyt to build a theater. Boxed between up-ended stone monoliths, the Red Rocks Theatre seats ten thousand people.

1517 Sand Dunes, San Luis Valley, Colorado

The Great Sand Dune District is now a National Monument   8A8

c. 1920

330 Great Sand Dunes, San Luis Valley, Colorado

Scene Showing "Lost River", Located on Edge of San Isabel National Forest   103052

c. 1920

In January 1807, Captain Zebulon Pike and his weary men—two with frozen feet—crossed the Sangre de Cristo Range and came upon an astonishing thousand-foot mountain formed by sand blowing across the San Luis Valley. Great Sand Dunes National Monument is an easy drive over La Veta Pass from Walsenburg.

c. 1945

c. 1910

c. 1910

c. 1910

c. 1910

Where They Dug the Gold

No passage in American history contains more courage, tragedy, humor, and folly than the Colorado gold and silver rushes which began in Denver in 1858. This drama of strikes and boom towns culminated in the Cripple Creek bonanza which reached its peak in 1900.

This mass yearning for riches filled Colorado with thousands of easterners who left their comfortable homes and went West to learn how to live in Colorado's thin air, how to grow food without much water, how to survive blizzards and bitter cold, and how to cook in a weird place where it took seven minutes to boil a six-minute egg. Instead of becoming discouraged by the hardships and returning to their warm eastern nests, the hardy stayed, making a place for themselves even in the harshness of the land.

The first gold rush was to the placer mines of Cherry Creek. Although those mines eventually petered out, rich, gold-bearing quartz was found at Gregory Gulch, creating the boomtowns of Central City, Black Hawk, Idaho Springs, and Gold Hill.

Those early strikes prompted even more prospectors to hurry to the Divide—to the London Mine at Fairplay, to Breckenridge and south to the Camp Bird Mine near Ouray, to the Tom Boy Mine at Telluride, and to the legendary Smuggler Mine at Aspen. Most frenzied of all, however, was the stampede in 1878 to Leadville, where silver lodes were found so rich that they caused the collapse of the world silver market in 1893.

People have always been fascinated by stories of gold rushes. The search for gold tantalizes not only because the dream of

Where gold was first discovered in Colo. on the Loop Trip, Colo. and So. Ry., Colo.

c. 1910

4160   AJAX MINE, CRIPPLE CREEK DISTRICT, COLO

c. 1910

finding it offers the potential of moving out of poverty into the world of luxury, power, and social prestige but also because nobody can predict when or where a gold strike will happen.

Such was the case when an amiable young cowman named Bob Womack insisted—to the point of boring his friends in Colorado Springs nearly to death—that there was a mountain of gold somewhere on the volcanic cone of Pikes Peak. The town was full of experienced prospectors who had combed every inch of Pikes Peak and knew for certain that there was no gold there. Bob did not argue with them except to remind them that gold is where you find it, not where it is supposed to be.

And in the fall of 1890, Bob Womack struck it rich at the head of a small stream which he called Cripple Creek because one of his cows injured herself trying to traverse the creek's steep bank. With gold nuggets in hand, Womack led his dubious friends to his cow pasture southwest of Pikes Peak—practically in the back yard of the present town of Colorado Springs—where they verified his claim. While the discovery made Womack a celebrity, it did little else for him. He was the kind of prospector who enjoyed the looking more than the finding. It was not long before he sold his pioneer El Paso Lode for $300—a mere fraction of its worth. But Cripple Creek was changed forever.

No longer a cow pasture, the town reached the amazing population of fifty thousand before the end of the 1890s, and its annual gold production came to half a billion dollars. For several years the Cripple Creek gold camp was known as the richest in the world. Much of the profit from all that gold went to Colorado Springs and its residents. One such resident was Winfield Scott Stratton, a carpenter who spent some of the millions of dollars from his mine, the Independence, to build the Stratton home for worthy indigents which still flourishes south of town today.

c. 1910

c. 1910

c. 1910

c. 1910

Ready for the Mines, Silverton, Colo.

c. 1905

2024   PROSPECTING IN THE MOUNTAINS, TRINIDAD, COLO.

c. 1905

1901   Placer Mining in Clear Creek Canon, Colo.
Colorado & Southern Ry.

c. 1910

SIGAFOOS TUNNELING MACHINE STARTING
ON CONTRACT AT GEORGETOWN, COLO.

c. 1910

8430. Bird's-Eye View of Black Hawk, Colo.

c. 1910

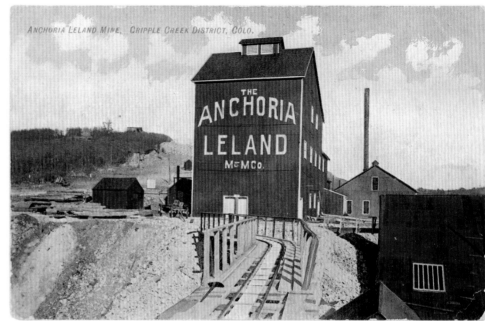

ANCHORIA LELAND MINE, CRIPPLE CREEK DISTRICT, COLO.

THE ANCHORIA LELAND McMCo.

c. 1910

Durant Mining Co., Aspen, Colo.

c. 1910

7207. Panning Gold

c. 1920

15544. Denver, Colorado, from State Capitol

c. 1920

1924. United States Mint and State Capitol, Denver, Colorado.

c. 1910

SCENE ON SIXTEENTH STREET, DENVER

c. 1905

118 CURTIS STREET AT NIGHT

DENVER, COLO.   5663-29

c. 1920

The Queen City

It is easy to understand why Denver happened to be built at the junction of Cherry Creek and the South Platte River on the Front Range of the Rockies: the site was only six hundred miles from civilization—in summer, just a ten-day ride on horseback over the flat prairie.

When farmers in Kansas heard that gold could be picked up in the sands at Cherry Creek, they hurried to the huddle of log cabins called Denver—named for James Denver, Governor of Kansas Territory, which became Colorado Territory in 1861.

It took years for the village of Denver to become a city—years of Indian troubles, crop failures, and the ups and downs of the mining business. But its pioneers provided strong leadership: the banker David M. Moffat; William M. Byers of the *Rocky Mountain News*; Walter Cheesman, who built Denver's water system; and John Evans, who by the 1870s had brought four railroads to the city and founded the University of Denver.

The city's growth was slow, but it picked up when Colorado advanced from territorial status to statehood on August 1, 1876—a date that accounts for its title as "The Centennial State." Denver's next period of growth, however, resulted from the riches pouring out of the town of Leadville, which created the endearing legend of Leadville's silver king, Horace A. W. Tabor, and his young dance hall mistress, whose romance was immortalized in the opera, "The Ballad of Baby Doe."

Tabor scattered his millions on Denver to make it, as he put it, "A city of elegance and refinement." In 1881, he built the Tabor

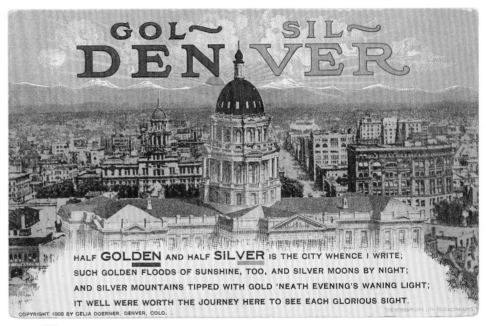

c. 1908

All aboard "Seeing Denver," Colorado.

c. 1910

Block and the Tabor Opera House, the most opulent theater in the West. When urged to hang Shakespeare's portrait in the Opera House lobby to upgrade the city's cultural standing, he demurred, asking, "What did Shakespeare ever do for Denver?"

But Tabor was best known for his scandalous marriage at age fifty-four to a ravishing twenty-eight-year-old divorcée from Oshkosh, Wisconsin, named Baby Doe McCourt. Baby Doe's wedding dress cost $7,500, and around her neck was a $90,000 diamond necklace. President Chester Alan Arthur and Senator Henry M. Teller from Colorado attended the wedding.

Thereafter, Tabor's fortunes plummeted until his death in 1899. But Baby Doe enhanced the Tabor legend immeasurably by her faithfulness to the memory of their love. During the bitter winter of 1935, she froze to death, penniless, in Leadville in a tiny log cabin near the Matchless Mine once owned by her late husband.

In 1896, the Colorado State Capitol, with its gold-plated dome, was completed on land donated by Henry C. Brown. In 1892, he built the Brown Palace Hotel, still Denver's most famous.

Then in 1904, Robert Walker Speer was elected mayor, and in just fifteen years he transformed the city into a metropolis. By cajolery and craft, he won the support of every faction in town—the moneyed aristocracy, city workers, bankers, bartenders, gamblers and Market Street madames. He beautified Cherry Creek by constructing Speer Boulevard alongside it. He built the grandiose Union Station, the Civic Center, the Denver Auditorium, and some forty charming city parks. He was also responsible for Red Rocks Park, the Daniels and Fisher Tower, and the United States Mint. In 1917, Speer boosted Denver's tourist business by negotiating the burial of Buffalo Bill Cody and his wife on nearby Lookout Mountain—despite the fact that the renowned scout was born in Iowa and spent his active years in Nebraska and Wyoming.

SIXTEENTH AND ARAPAHOE STREETS, DENVER, COLO.

c. 1905

c. 1910

EQUITABLE BUILDING, DENVER, COLO.

c. 1905

c. 1910

c. 1910

c. 1910

c. 1910

c. 1920

1780. Union Station, Denver, Colo.

c. 1910

200 Rooms, Fire Proof, Modern in every Detail. Three Cafes, Cuisine and Service Par Excellence.

Popular Prices Prevail Throughout the House. No Charge for Transferring Baggage from and to Union Depot. THE HAMILTON-BROOKS CO.

WELCOME   OXFORD HOTEL

The Welcome Arch, Denver; the Oxford Hotel and 17th. St. at Union Depot.

c. 1910

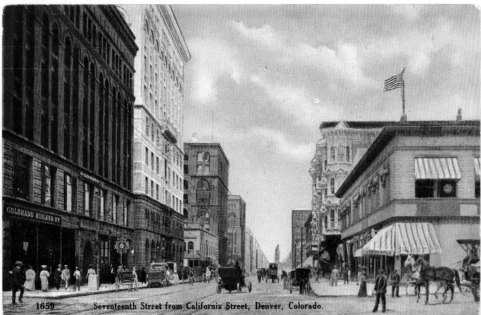

1659   Seventeenth Street from California Street, Denver, Colorado.

c. 1910

In the early 1900s, the sleek passenger trains of seven major railroads brought millions of visitors to marvel at Denver's palatial station. The splendor and gargantuan size of the "Welcome" which greeted them as they left their train at Union Station said a lot about the perennial optimism that still inspires the residents of Denver.

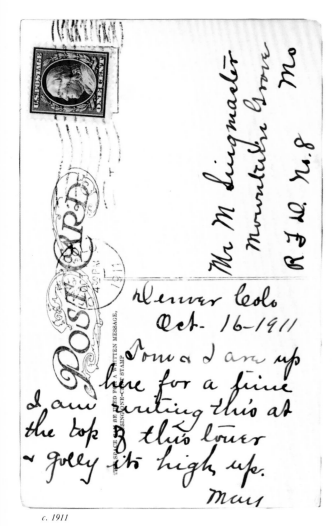

c. 1911

7577   The Daniels & Fisher Stores Co., Denver, Colo.
Established Oct. 6, 1864.
Height of Tower, 330 Feet.

c. 1911

THE BROWN PALACE HOTEL, DENVER

c. 1935

Built in the early 1900s, the 375-foot Daniels and Fisher Tower was modeled on Venice's Campanile of St. Mark's. Its bell rang out the news of President Taft's election, and its tower housed Denver's first airport beacon.

c. 1913

c. 1910

c. 1913

c. 1905

c. 1905

This old plug has a high place in Denver history as the "horse power" of the city's first street car. The rails were laid so that Old Dobbin could pull the car up the hill and then ride in the vestibule as the car coasted down. With the importance of livestock in the early 1900s, meat packing and feed selling were major industries in Denver.

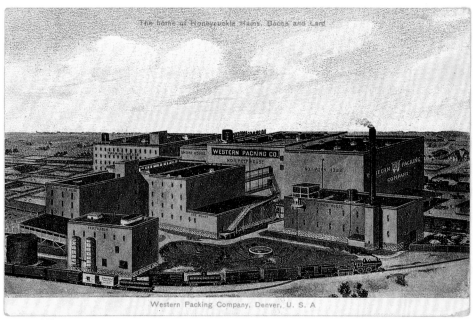

c. 1905

7662. Denver Dry Goods Co. Building
400 Feet Long—7 Acres Floor Area
Sixteenth and California and Fifteenth Streets
Denver, Colorado

c. 1910

LEADING CONFECTIONERY IN THE WEST.
GEO. ALLISON. 1011-15TH ST.,   DENVER, COLO.

c. 1905

ARAPAHOE BUTTER SHOP

DENVER DAIRY CO.

1037 15. ST.   1035

THE ARAPAHOE BRAND   THE ARAPAHOE BUTTER SHOP

c. 1910

THE NANKING
First Class American and Chinese Restaurant
CHOP SUEY
1712 Curtis St., Denver, Colo.

c. 1910

"THE TEPEES" 18 MILES WEST OF DENVER, COLORADO   Bring your SQUAW up Sometime.

c. 1945

c. 1945

c. 1945

EXCELLO SANDWICH SHOP — 1659 CURTIS ST., 1008 17th ST. — DENVER, COLO.

c. 1945

c. 1945

THE BEACON SUPPER CLUB

Never Too Busy To Say Hello

"Willie" Hartzell

"Jerry" Bakke

BEACON SUPPER CLUB

WORLD FAMOUS MUSIC

7800 East Colfax

Denver, Colorado

c. 1945

STAPLETON MUNICIPAL AIRPORT, DENVER, COLORADO

c. 1945

2039—Lowry Field Hangars and Barracks, Denver, Colorado

U. S. ARMY

"OFFICIAL LOWRY FIELD PHOTO"

c. 1945

Denver, Colo. The Miss Wolcott School.

ST. ROSA'S HOME FOR WORKING GIRLS, DENVER, COLORADO.

c. 1920

DENVER UNIVERSITY CAMPUS, DENVER, COLO.

c. 1910

FOOTE HALL, COLORADO WOMAN'S COLLEGE, DENVER, COLORADO

c. 1940

106—Public Library and North Section of the Civic Center, Denver, Colorado City and County Building in Background

c. 1940

c. 1910

There is little hope for people just half trained

Accredited Member,
American Association of Commercial Colleges

Our New Building
We Pay No Rent

Logan at Colfax

Parks School of Business Administration, Denver, Colo.

One Block East of the Capitol

c. 1930

WEST HIGH SCHOOL WITH SUNKEN GARDEN IN FOREGROUND . . . DENVER, COLORADO

c. 1940

AN OFFICE MACHINE CLASS—CENTRAL BUSINESS COLLEGE
1177 GRANT STREET, DENVER, COLORADO

c. 1945

1266. Elmwood School, Denver.

c. 1905

1863   Boathouse and Ball Room, Lakeside Park, White City, Denver, Colorado.

c. 1910

ROCKET SHIPS — LAKESIDE PARK — DENVER, COLO.

c. 1945

LOBBY OF THE FAMOUS ELITCH GARDENS THEATRE

DENVER, COLO.   117087-N

c. 1925

Since 1890, Denver residents have enjoyed times at amusement parks such as Elitch Gardens, which featured scary rides and a theater. Later, the Lakeside Amusement Park highlighted speed boat racing, rides, and games.

c. 1920

The architecture of the Colorado State Capitol, completed in 1908 at a cost of $3,492,744, is "Greek Corinthian." In its rotunda are eight murals by Allen True embellished with poetry by Thomas Hornsby Ferril, the state's poet laureate.

c. 1910

c. 1910

123—Colorado Museum of Natural History, Overlooking City Park, Denver, Colorado

c. 1940

1667. Shady Lane, City Park, Denver, Colorado.

c. 1910

7427 Public Play Grounds, Denver, Colorado

c. 1910

15223. Lily Pond, City Park, Denver, Colo.

c. 1915

8006. Fort Collins Automobile Club,
Fort Collins, Colo,

c. 1910

5—Sewing Class, Colorado Agricultural College.

c. 1905

Eaton High School & Grade School
in the distance.

c. 1910

810—Business District, Ft. Collins, Colorado, Showing Intersection of Mountain,

College Avenues and Linden Street

c. 1930

The Front Range

The words "Front Range" refer to a strip of land on the eastern edge of the Rocky Mountains that is 30 miles wide and extends for 276 miles from the Wyoming border south to New Mexico's Raton Pass. The strip has "humps" reaching elevations of up to seventy-three hundred feet. One hump between Denver and Colorado Springs, notorious for the ferocious storms which occur there without warning, sends motorists fleeing to lower ground for safety. One-third of all Coloradans live on this strip in a dozen towns that struggle to keep from being gobbled up by their aggressive neighbor, Denver.

Fort Collins, just south of the Wyoming border, began in 1864 as an army post erected to guard travelers along the California Trail. Its farmers prospered on crops watered by the Cache la Poudre River, and Colorado State University was founded there in 1870. The state has benefited from the university's research in animal husbandry, veterinary medicine, forestry, computer science, and control of Rocky Mountain tick fever.

Financed by Horace Greeley of *The New York Tribune* and managed by Nathan Meeker who was one of his writers, the city of Greeley, also on the Cache la Poudre River, began in 1870 as a socialist community of "proper persons"—meaning no drinkers. The settlers invented a system of irrigation that was adopted throughout Colorado, bringing such prosperity to the city that its citizens gave up socialism and became capitalists.

Near Greeley is Loveland, called "The Sweetheart Town" because of its heart-shaped postmark which is stamped on thousands

Gathering Wild Flowers on Cripple Creek Auto Route, Colorado, Pikes Peak in distance.

c. 1925

COMMERCIAL STREET, LOOKING NORTH FROM MAIN STREET, SIMPSON'S REST IN DISTANCE,

TRINIDAD, COLORADO.

c. 1925

of valentines every year. The nearby city of Longmont is named for Longs Peak, which towers above both the city and the scenic canyon that provides entry to the Rocky Mountain National Park.

The most fertile part of the Front Range strip stretches from Denver north for some sixty miles through Boulder, Greeley, and Fort Collins. Its green croplands almost resemble Iowa because of irrigation water brought from the western slope by transmontane tunnels such as the Colorado-Big Thompson system. In the 1930s, the Moffat Tunnel tapped the Blue River near the Dillon Reservoir, bringing to Denver the water that made possible the true beginning of its metropolitan expansion.

The University of Colorado at Boulder and the Colorado School of Mines at Golden were both authorized by the Territorial Legislature in 1861, but funds to operate the University of Colorado were not provided until 1876, when construction was begun on a picturesque 587-acre site at the base of Flagstaff Mountain.

Colorado Springs was founded in 1871 by General William Jackson Palmer, a Civil War cavalry hero. It was the first resort in the West devoted purely to pleasure. The improvement of health and tourism were its main concerns through the 1930s. Then in 1941, the city was overwhelmed by military installations—Fort Carson, the Consolidated Air Defense Command (NORAD), and later, the Space Center for the Strategic Defense Initiative. The military influx attracted so many high-tech companies to Colorado Springs from California's "Silicon Valley" that people suggested changing the name of Pikes Peak to "Silicon Mountain."

The Front Range strip south of Pueblo was settled by Spanish-speaking pioneers long before the Anglos joined the gold rush to Denver in 1859. Those same pioneers from New Mexico founded in 1852 the town of San Luis in the San Luis Valley—making it the first community in what would become the state of Colorado.

FOURTH STREET, LOOKING WEST, LOVELAND, COLORADO

c. 1945

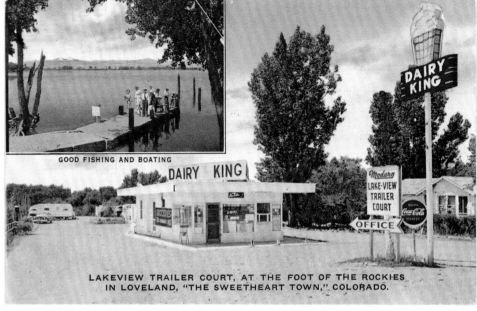

GOOD FISHING AND BOATING

LAKEVIEW TRAILER COURT, AT THE FOOT OF THE ROCKIES
IN LOVELAND, "THE SWEETHEART TOWN," COLORADO.

c. 1920

CENTRAL PRESBYTERIAN CHURCH AND CARNEGIE LIBRARY, LONGMONT, COLORADO.

c. 1945

9210. Greeley Fire Department, Greeley, Colo.

c. 1910

c. 1910

Beautiful Boulder Canyon Highway runs from Boulder—an 1859 gold-rush center—to the mining town of Nederland. The Scott Carpenter Park, named for the famous astronaut born in Boulder, is a popular recreation area.

15211. Pearl Street Looking East, Boulder, Colorado

c. 1920

Boulder, Colorado from Mount Flagstaff

c. 1910

Public Library,
Boulder,
Colorado

c. 1910

COLORADO UNIVERSITY STADIUM
UNIVERSITY OF COLORADO
BOULDER, COLO.

PUB. by FINE & COULSON

c. 1910

737—Campus and Prexy's Walk.
Campus of the University of Colorado
at Boulder

c. 1940

727 BOULDER COUNTY COURT HOUSE

BOULDER, COLO.

4A157

c. 1930

608. Eldorado Springs, Colo.   Ivy Baldwin on the Tight Rope.
Height, 582 feet.   Length, 530 feet.

c. 1910

c. 1910

Swimming Pool, Eldorado Springs, Colorado.

c. 1910

c. 1910

c. 1915

c. 1950

c. 1915

In the famous bar of the Teller House, Denver's Herndon Davis was inspired to paint Challis Walker's face on the barroom floor. Word of the face has spread world-wide, and draws at least as many people to Central City as the opera.

5993. Golden, Colorado, and Entrance to Clear Creek Canon, from Castle Rock Mountain Scenic Incline Railway. DENVER MOUNTAIN PARKS.

©WISWALL

c. 1910

Territorial Governor John Evans and railroad man W. A. H. Loveland feuded over whether Denver or Golden should become Colorado's capital. Evans brought railroads from Kansas and Wyoming, resulting in victory for Denver.

8191 Castle Rock and Adolph Coor's Golden Brewery, Golden, Colo.

c. 1915

BIRD'S EYE VIEW OF GOLDEN, COLO. BY NIGHT.

c. 1920

c. 1910

c. 1940

c. 1910

Maintained as a museum by the Colorado Historical Society, Leadville's Healy House was built in 1878 by a rich miner. Cripple Creek was named by Bob Womack in 1890 because a cow broke its leg while crossing the creek. The view from Buena Vista takes in the Collegiate Range of fourteen-thousand footers—Princeton, Yale, and Harvard.

5645. Pavilion, Cave of the Winds, Manitou Springs, Colo.

c. 1920

544—Alcove in the Valley of Dreams, Cave of the Winds, Manitou Springs, Colo.

c. 1930

A tourist attraction near Manitou Springs, the Cave of the Winds consists of many underground rooms of stalactites and stalagmites hollowed out of the limestone by underground waters. One of the cave's chambers is called "Old Maids' Kitchen" because legend has it that if a girl leaves a hairpin there she can expect to be married within a year.

7839 Navajo Geyser Pavilion and Hotel Navajo, Manitou, Colo.
In center of Manitou, opposite the Soda Springs Park. Superior location, table and
service. American and European Plan. **$2.50 and Up Per Day, $15.00 and
up Per Week, American** and $1.00 and up Per Night, European. Special rates for two or
more occupying one room.

The undersigned, Denver representative for the "NAVAJO" will be glad to call and
name rates for individuals and parties.

JOHN C. POLLEN,
Hotel Lafayette, Denver

c. 1910

15338 - ROTUNDA, MANITOU SPRINGS BATH HOUSE,
MANITOU SPRINGS, COLORADO.

c. 1930

DELICIOUS IRON
WATER LEMONADE
"TRY IT"

4051   UTE IRON SPRINGS, MANITOU, COLORADO.   SHOWING FOUNTAIN BUILT OF NATIVE MINERAL SPECIMENS.

c. 1930

Grand View Hotel, Manitou, Colo.

GRAND VIEW

c. 1910

8394. Pike's Peak Avenue and Antlers Hotel, Colorado Springs, Colo.

Tejon Street, Colorado Springs, Colo.

c. 1910

7103. Bird's Eye View of Colorado Springs, Colo.

Alamo Hotel.   Antlers Hotel.   Exchange Nat. Bank Bldg.

c. 1910

7461. Congress Hotel, Pueblo, Colo.

c. 1910

Pikes Peak from Colorado Springs, Colo. Midland Ry., Colo.

c. 1910

c. 1910

c. 1910

c. 1910

c. 1909

c. 1910

107. Cathedral Spires, Garden of the Gods.

c. 1905

100. Gateway to the Garden of the Gods, Colorado

c. 1905

145—Balanced Rock and Steamboat Rock,
Western Gateway Garden of the Gods

c. 1905

© JOHN O'BYRNE

c. 1914

Chasing the Cure   M. W. of A. Sanatorium

c. 1910

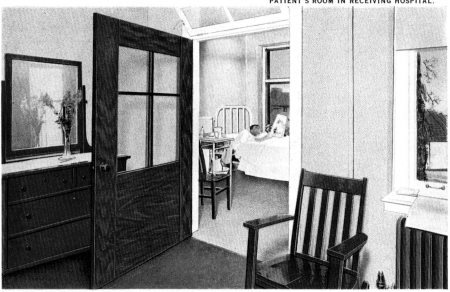

PATIENT'S ROOM IN RECEIVING HOSPITAL.

MODERN WOODMEN OF AMERICA SANATORIUM, WOODMEN, COLO.   103972

c. 1925

8062. "THE TICKLER" LAKESIDE, DENVER.

c. 1909

DIET KITCHEN FOR HOSPITAL PATIENTS.

MODERN WOODMEN OF AMERICA SANATORIUM, WOODMEN, COLO.   103969

c. 1925

1942. Main Street, looking east, Florence, Colo.

c. 1910

7814. Skyline Drive, Canon City, Colorado. *On the D. & R. G. W. R. R.*

c. 1920

State Penitentiary, Canon City, Colorado.

c. 1910

Alpine Park Salida.

c. 1910

SOLDIERS' AND SAILORS' CLUB, PUEBLO, COLO.

c. 1920

14—Colorado Fuel and Iron Company, Minnequa Steel Works, Pueblo, Colo.

Pueblo, a Thriving City with a Lasting Prosperity

63117-C-N

c. 1920

5022.   Union Ave. Bridge Over Arkansas River, Pueblo, Colo.

c. 1910

Corner Fourth and Main St., Pueblo, Col.

c. 1910

MINERAL PALACE HOME OF THE EIGHTEENTH NATIONAL IRRIGATION CONGRESS PUEBLO, COLORADO, SEPTEMBER 26-30, 1910

c. 1910

INTERIOR VIEW, SHOWING "SILVER QUEEN" AND "KING COAL," MINERAL PALACE, PUEBLO, COLO.

c. 1910

Scene on Lake Clara, Pueblo, Colo.

c. 1910

COLORADO STATE FLAG, MINERAL PALACE PARK, PUEBLO, COLO.

c. 1910

1585—Monument Lake Fish Hatchery, Monument Lake Park, near Trinidad, Colo.

8A301-N

c. 1925

Mount Blanca, 14,464 ft. high, near Blanca, Colo.

c. 1905

1519 Main Street, Alamosa, Colorado

The Business Center of the Great San Luis Valley

8A266

c. 1930

Discovered in 1779 by Juan Bautista de Anza, Blanca Peak, with an altitude of 14,317 feet, is the fourth highest peak of the Rocky Mountain Range and is one of the most beautiful. One of de Anza's priests, noting the mountains' ruddy color at sunrise, named the whole range *Sangre de Cristo*, which is translated "Blood of Christ."

c. 1910

c. 1905

c. 1910

c. 1910

c. 1910

The Western Slope

The residents of Colorado's country west of the Continental Divide have a tendency to look down on those eager beavers in the cities of the Front Range.

The inhabitants of the western slope are wary of the easterners' habit of siphoning their precious Colorado River water across the Divide through transmountain tunnels to sustain Weld County farms and the suburbs of Denver. Some of the western slope's Eagle River water is also delivered by tunnel to the Arkansas River, which supplies the cities of Pueblo and Colorado Springs.

The westerners envy the fame enjoyed by the easterners for the romantic exploits of Baby Doe Tabor and the Unsinkable Molly Brown, who survived the Titanic disaster in 1912. But the westerners have their stories, too, such as the tale of Alfred Packer, who in 1873 ate five of his frozen friends in Lake City. A partisan judge sentenced Packer with the words, "They was seven Democrats in Hinsdale County and you ate five of them. Stand up you man-eatin' so-and-so and take your punishment."

A second Western Slope tale involves Marshall Pass. Named for William L. Marshall, who lived in Silverton, Marshall Pass has an altitude of 10,846 feet. Legend tells us that William had a toothache so bad that he hastened to his dentist in Denver by a crow's-flight route instead of the longer stage coach road. He found and crossed the then-unknown pass, thereby saving himself 125 miles of rough stage road and four hours of toothache misery.

The easterners can talk of their Sand Creek Indian Massacre in 1864 at Chivington near Lamar. But the westerners had their

c. 1940

historic massacre, too. In 1879, near what later became the town of Meeker, the White River Ute Indians killed thirty white men to protest the gold seekers' trespasses on their hunting grounds. In retribution, the United States Senate revoked the Indians' title to most of the western slope of Colorado, which they had occupied since pre-Columbian times. The Utes were subsequently moved to small reservations in Utah and southwest Colorado.

Their departure caused a stampede of homesteaders over the Divide and the founding of Durango, Gunnison, Montrose, and Grand Junction. Pagosa Springs was started later, a unique resort whose homes and public buildings were heated in winter by its hot springs water. Glenwood Springs, another natural hot springs, still uses its water in an outdoor pool where visitors can swim—with the air temperature at 40 degrees below zero. The Colorado Hotel in Glenwood Springs was built in 1891 by Walter Devereux—a polo enthusiast from Long Island—who sent polo players from the hotel to promote the game in Colorado Springs and Denver.

Besides its star polo players, the Colorado Hotel won further renown in January 1901 when Vice President Theodore Roosevelt spent a week there en route to hunt "cougars"—mountain lions—at the Keystone Ranch north of Meeker. Back at the hotel later, he reported that he had killed a 227-pound cougar—and sent the skin to the Smithsonian Museum in Washington, D.C.

Founded as a result of a silver boom in 1879, Aspen's great days as a winter sports capital did not begin until 1941, when Camp Hale was established to train combat skiers for the United States Army. That led to a ski resort at Aspen when Walter C. Paepcke gave the city the longest—three miles—and fastest chair lift in the world. More ski centers came to Vail, Steamboat Springs, and many other high places on the western slope, making Colorado one of the best known of all centers for the sport.

Ready to break Camp. Scene on the Colorado Midland Ry.

c. 1910

14927 GENERAL VIEW OF GRAND RIVER VALLEY, COLO. SHOWING GRAND JUNCTION IN DISTANCE. DETROIT PUBLISHING CO

c. 1910

Fifth Street, Grand Junction, Colo.

c. 1920

6110 Panorama of Palisade, Colorado.

c. 1910

31. Durango, Colorado.

c. 1905

Main Avenue, Durango, Colo.   Pub. by J. O. Taylor.

c. 1910

THE CHIEF DINER
"For Fine Foods"
DURANGO, COLORADO

c. 1940

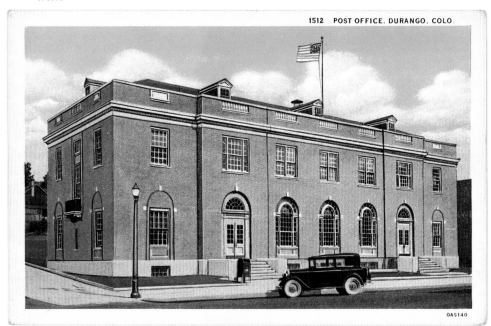

1512   POST OFFICE, DURANGO, COLO.

c. 1930

c. 1910

c. 1910

c. 1910

In 1892, Bob Ford, that "dirty little coward," shot Jesse James in the back in the colorful gold-camp town of Creede. And later, Soapy Smith took over the town "lock, stock and parlor house," as Perry Eberhart phrased it.

AURAY, CHIEF OF THE UTE NATION.

E. C. KROPP, PUBL., MILWAUKEE NO. 232.

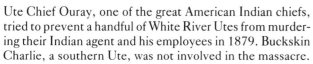

c. 1905

233. Ute Children.

c. 1905

203—Chief Buckskin Charlie
and Squaw.

c. 1905

Ute Chief Ouray, one of the great American Indian chiefs, tried to prevent a handful of White River Utes from murdering their Indian agent and his employees in 1879. Buckskin Charlie, a southern Ute, was not involved in the massacre.

c. 1930

c. 1930

c. 1935

c. 1940

8465. Union Depot, Track View, Denver, Colo.

c. 1910

INTERIOR OF NEW TYPE DINING CAR ON THE COLUMBINE. FLOWER OF TRAVEL COMFORT.
NAMED IN HONOR OF COLORADO'S STATE FLOWER

c. 1930

"FRONTIER SHACK" ON THE STREAMLINER "CITY OF DENVER"

c. 1930

MOFFAT TUNNEL, COLORADO

MOFFAT TUNNEL 1923 1927

c. 1940

Soaring Rails

Nothing in the story of Colorado is more amazing than the building of its four thousand miles of railroads. They were pushed to serve every high mine along the Continental Divide that had as much as "a shirt-tail full of ore," as the hard-rock miners put it.

In 1872, John Evans, Colorado's territorial Governor, plunged deep into the "inaccessible" Rockies across the Continental Divide. An iron-willed man, Evans headed toward the remote gold camps of Gunnison and Pitkin. Following General W. J. Palmer's example, he adopted the narrow gauge—thirty-six inches—instead of the usual forty-eight inches between rails. General Palmer had used this gauge in 1871 for the route followed by his Denver and Rio Grande Railroad because it allowed turns so sharp that the locomotive could pass its own caboose. While the narrow gauge did allow for sharp turns, there were problems: Palmer's trains were so light the wind could blow them off the track.

By bull-headed persistence, Evans pushed his railroad over Kenosha Pass to the Upper Arkansas River, then up Chalk Creek to St. Elmo. Near Tincup, the road went through the Alpine Tunnel under Altman Pass and on to Gunnison. Then in 1880, Evans sold the railroad to Jay Gould, who soon after sold it to the Union Pacific. The Union Pacific branched off from the Evans line at Como and made it to Leadville over Boreas Pass and the 11,320-foot Fremont Pass—its second crossing of the Divide.

Meanwhile, with a construction force larger than the entire United States Army in the 1880s, General Palmer flung the spidery

c. 1910

rails of his Denver and Rio Grande Railroad into the San Luis Valley over La Veta Pass, and then to Durango via Cumbres Pass and Toltec Gorge. From Salida, Palmer's trains went over Marshall Pass and through the mile-deep Black Canyon of the Gunnison River to Grand Junction. But gun-toting employees of the Santa Fe Railroad contested the Denver and Rio Grande route through the Royal Gorge to Leadville. In the court fight that ensued, the Santa Fe Railroad lost when the judge awarded the right-of-way through the Royal Gorge to General Palmer.

The Denver and Rio Grande, however, had a more serious rival. In 1887, James J. Hagerman, finding business in Colorado Springs "as dead as Julius Caesar," decided to stir things up at Pikes Peak. His Colorado Midland Railroad went up the "impossible" 7 percent grade of Ute Pass and over Hagerman Pass above Leadville, then on as far as Rifle.

Deep snows kept the Colorado Midland from operating in winter, but that did not deter others from building railroads into the stratosphere. In 1902, David Moffat, the richest and most powerful man in Colorado, built his Moffat Railroad from Denver over Rollins Pass (altitude 11,680 feet) and on through Gore Canyon for 550 miles to Steamboat Springs and Craig. Because the winter snows almost ended the career of the Moffat Road, William G. Evans, the son of John Evans, persuaded the City of Denver in 1928 to build the Moffat Tunnel—over six miles long and costing almost fifteen and one-half million dollars. The tunnel saved the railroad 2,421 feet of climb and put the tracks at 9,259 feet, well below the deep snow altitude. Today, the old Corona Pass route remains one of the most terrifying auto roads in Colorado, and the Moffat Tunnel continues to serve both the Moffat Road and the short-cut route of the Denver and Rio Grande Railroad from Denver to Glenwood Springs.

Arrow, Colo., on the Moffat Road.

c. 1910

8678. Looping the Loop, Denver, Northwestern & Pacific, "The Moffat Road," Colo.

6749. DEVIL'S SLIDE ON THE C. S. & C. C. SHORT LINE, COLO.

c. 1901

1853. Inspiration Point, Clear Creek Canon, Colorado.
Colorado & Southern Ry.

c. 1910

7041. Zig Zag Climb to Mt. McClellan, Colo., 6% Grade, Argentine Central Ry.

c. 1910

The terrifying Colorado Springs and Cripple Creek Railroad (1901-1915) was only forty-six miles long, but as Vice President Theodore Roosevelt said when he rode it in April 1901, "This railroad bankrupts the English language!"

6173   A. T. & S. F. Railway Shops, La Junta, Colo.

c. 1910

1544.   Yankee Doodle Lake, on the Moffat Road, Colorado.

c. 1910

Near Point Sublime the Cripple Creek, Short Line, Colo.

c. 1910

Today, Point Sublime can be reached by car in the summer on the Gold Camp Road, formerly the railroad right-of-way. At Yankee Doodle Lake, the Moffat Road added extra engines to cross the 11,680-foot Rollins Pass.

9058. ROYAL GORGE, COLORADO.   COPYRIGHT, 1905, BY DETROIT PHOTOGRAPHIC CO.

c. 1905

8228. South Platte River, in South Park, on Colo. Midland Ry.

c. 1910

OPEN TOP OBSERVATION CAR
AT THE HANGING BRIDGE IN ROYAL GORGE,
GRAND CANON OF THE ARKANSAS, COLORADO.
ON THE DENVER AND RIO GRANDE RAILROAD.

c. 1910

1881   Forks of the Creek, Clear Creek Canon, Colorado.   *Colorado & Southern Ry.*

REFRESHMENTS

c. 1910

c. 1910

c. 1930

c. 1930

In 1880, the Denver and Rio Grande Railroad was built from Canon City to Leadville through the Royal Gorge. Later, motorists found a thrill in crossing the Royal Gorge Bridge a thousand feet above the Arkansas River.

FIRST NATIONAL BANK, LAMAR, COLORADO.

c. 1925

H-1965 OLD HOME OF KIT CARSON NEAR LAS ANIMAS, COLORADO

c. 1925

CAMPSITE OF THE FAMOUS INDIAN SCOUT "KIT CARSON" — KIT CARSON, COLORADO

152 MILES EAST OF DENVER — **498** MILES WEST OF KANSAS CITY — ON HIGHWAY U. S. 40-S.

c. 1925

ALFALFA FIELD, TYPICAL OF WESTERN KANSAS AND EASTERN COLORADO

c. 1945

The High Plains

Almost half of Colorado lies in the undulating eastern plains, sometimes called "short grass country" or "the land of tall skies." These plains spread westward from the border of Kansas for one hundred fifty miles to the Front Range at the twin Spanish Peaks.

In the 1870s, the land along the Arkansas and South Platte rivers was controlled by cattle barons who grazed their Texas longhorns free on the unfenced plains. But in the 1880s, their control of the grasslands ended when land-hungry farmers took homesteads in eastern Colorado and tried dry-land farming. Their success resulted in the founding of pleasant towns like Holyoke, Wray, Yucca, Akron, and Lamar—called the "Goose Capital of America" because of its popularity with goose hunters.

The dry-land farmers of the late 1800s endured years of hardship caused by water shortages, grasshopper plagues, tornadoes, summer dust storms, and winter blizzards. But by the 1900s, they had come to love their difficult environment with its limitless horizon and azure skies that made other places seem cramped and colorless. Most of all, they were sustained by the spirit of cooperation that animates the plains people to this day. Together, they have built irrigation systems for their livestock and their wheat and corn crops. Recently, many dry-land farmers have begun to use huge circular sprinklers, drawing water from the vast Ogallala aquifer underlying the eastern high plains.

The largest of the High Plains cities is the farmer's supply center of Sterling, on the South Platte River. Sterling began in the 1880s

H-1013   FIELD OF WHEAT NEAR LA JUNTA, COLORADO.

c. 1930

with the arrival of the railroads. Fifteen miles south of Sterling is the Summit Springs Battlefield. On July 11, 1869, federal troops from Kansas were sent into Colorado to rescue two white women reported to have been taken captive by a band of Cheyenne Indians under Tall Bull. In the day-long battle that was the last military engagement between soldiers and Indians on the High Plains of Colorado, the Indians were defeated, but the two women were casualties.

A major historical site on the Arkansas River a few miles from La Junta is the huge, splendidly restored Bent's Fort, administered by the National Park Service. The Fort was built in 1828 by the four Bent brothers and their partner, Ceran St. Vrain, all of whom were leading actors in the development of the fur trade and in the role of United States troops in guarding the Santa Fe Trail. The Fort was the favorite rendezvous for Kit Carson, Bill Williams, and all the famous mountain men during 1841 and 1842. It was John Charles Fremont's base when he was en route to California in 1845. Colonel Kearney also stopped there in 1846 with his army on his way to bring New Mexico into the United States.

The lively town of Rocky Ford began in 1878 when a farmer, George W. Swink, discovered that watermelons would thrive on irrigation water from the Arkansas River. Swink invited his friends to participate in Watermelon Day, which is still held as a feature of the Arkansas Valley Fair during the third week in August. More than ten thousand free watermelons are given to those attending. In addition to pride in its watermelons, the town also claims to be the world's largest grower of Zinnia seeds.

Ten miles up the Arkansas River from La Junta, the Santa Fe trains fork off to cross Raton Pass on the way to Albuquerque and Los Angeles. La Junta is headquarters for the Koshare Indian Dancers, Explorer Scouts who perform for tourists each summer.

Dinner Time, Wray Colo.

c. 1910

Bird's-Eye View   Fort Morgan, Colo.

c. 1910

Dryland Farm.   Morgan County, Colo.

c. 1910

1607. Irrigation in Northern Colorado.

c. 1925

Edison Street, looking East, Brush, Colo.

c. 1910

c. 1940

c. 1914

c. 1940

STREET SCENE, ROCKY FORD, COLORADO

c. 1935

H-2857. SANTA FE HOTEL, LA JUNTA, COLORADO.

c. 1930

St. Patrick's Church, La Junta, Colo.

c. 1910

Eastern motorists sometimes neglect the High Plains in their rush to get into the Rockies, but the flatland towns have their own special charm. Summer brings to La Junta the performances of a Koshare Indian Boy Scout troop.

Horticultural Display, Colorado, New Mexico... Fair at Durango, Colorado.

c. 1910

Street Scene on Melon Day, Rocky Ford, Colo.

c. 1910

Marketing Sugar Beets, Delta, Colo.

c. 1910

127 (Before the Feast.) Melon Day, Rocky Ford, Colo. Copyright by P. E. Kennedy.

c. 1905

Bounty and Celebrations

The people of Colorado have never let their work interfere with the business of having a good time. Even the early miners set aside their prospecting in order to "see the elephant" in the dance halls of Denver and Central City.

The state's paramount interest in outdoor sports and recreation dates back to 1891, when President Benjamin Harrison was authorized by Congress to set aside a National Forest Preserve near Colorado Springs—the first step in the nation's conservation policy. That first reserve became today's Pike National Forest. Later, President Theodore Roosevelt gave the reserve policy official status by creating the United States Forest Service under the Department of Agriculture. Thereafter, Roosevelt created so many national forests that today some twenty million square miles of Colorado, including parks, monuments, and B.L.M. acreage, belongs to the federal government.

All through the early 1900s, President Roosevelt's frequent hunting trips in Colorado prompted local residents to make use of federal lands—to stalk deer in White River National Forest or elk in Uncompahgre National Forest. Trout fishermen then went on to discover Gunnison National Forest, while duck hunters went to the forests near San Luis Valley. The Colorado Mountain Club—including some members who have climbed all fifty-three of the state's peaks that are over fourteen thousand feet—was organized to take advantage of the national forests.

In the 1940s, the allotment of national forests for skiers' use brought about a new industry. The explosive growth that brought

ROUNDING UP CATTLE ON JACK RABBITS IN THE WEST—M2

c. 1940

annually a million skiers to the state resulted from huge investments in fifty thousand square miles of ski country and deluxe accommodations at Aspen, Vail, Breckenridge, Crested Butte, and a dozen other resorts along the Continental Divide. Their popularity owed much to the Colorado Highway Department for keeping the roads open and safe under winter conditions.

Coloradans have always created entertainment to fit their way of life. The Colorado State Fair and Industrial Exposition has been a major event in late August since 1900. Besides horse racing and cattle exhibits, it boasts in recent years of having "the world's largest rabbit show." The big winter event is the National Western Stock Show, which began in 1899 and has been attended by stockmen from around the world. They assemble for business but also find time for horseplay such as parking $50,000 prize Hereford bulls in the dignified lobby of the Brown Palace Hotel.

Colorado has always had summer day festivals beloved by farmers and ranchers, such as Pumpkin Pie Day in Longmont and Strawberry Day in Glenwood Springs. Of the August rodeos, the largest is the Pikes Peak or Bust Rodeo in Colorado Springs. It is kicked off with a free outdoor breakfast on Pikes Peak Avenue for twenty thousand people. Among several notable Colorado melodramas, the longest-running has been staged summers since 1948 at the Imperial Hotel in Cripple Creek.

Colorado's most celebrated cultural event is the Aspen Music Festival, which began in 1949. In addition to its public performances, the festival draws famous writers and musicians to the Aspen Institute for Humanistic Studies.

Historically, golf in Colorado dates back to 1891, when the second golf course in the United States (the first was at Yonkers, New York, in 1888) was laid out at the Cheyenne Mountain Country Club in Colorado Springs.

PILES OF WATERMELONS AT ROCKY FORD FAIR GROUNDS
ROCKY FORD, COLORADO

c. 1940

1611. Wheat Field, Northern Colorado.

c. 1925

Old Mill (oldest in the State),
Littleton, Colo.

c. 1910

FRUIT DRYING, MONTROSE, COLO.

c. 1910

1609. Lamb Feeding in Northern Colorado.

c. 1925

Colo. is the place we grow large cabbage.

c. 1908

c. 1908

c. 1908

Hauling sugar beets in Colo.

c. 1909

c. 1910

c. 1910

c. 1910

During the early part of the century, well-attended summer Chautauquas were held in many Colorado cities, providing enjoyable cultural advancement as well as culinary events. In Longmont, the summer highlight was Pumpkin Pie Day.

7106. Bird's Eye View of Grand Valley Orchards, Colo.

c. 1910

13605 PICKING APPLES, CANON CITY, COLO.

c. 1930

In the Canon City and Paonis areas and along the Rio Grande above Grand Junction, summer's cool nights and moderate daytime temperatures favored the growing of fruits. But orchards often needed heat by late September.

Heating an Orchard, Grand Junction, Colo.

c. 1910

c. 1910

2806 Threshing Grain in the Hilly Country of the West,

c. 1909

c. 1907

When the hunting season opens, residents and non-residents by the thousands obtain hunting licenses and head for the country deep in the mountains, where antelope, bear, mountain goat, Rocky Mountain sheep, turkey, grouse, pheasant, and quail are plentiful. Or they hunt the migrating ducks that pause at the reservoirs on their way south.

LARIMER COUNTY FAIR AND RODEO LOVELAND, COLO.

c. 1910

B6118   Bull-dogging a Steer, Cattleman's Day, Gunnison, Colo.

c. 1910

DOC THORN HUNTING A SOFT SPOT, MONTE VISTA STAMPEDE, (COPYRIGHT 1919, R.R. DOUBLEDAY)

c. 1910

EDUCATED BRAHMA OWNED AND TRAINED BY KNUTE JOHNSON, LONGMONT, COLO.

c. 1910

c. 1913

c. 1913

c. 1913

c. 1910

c. 1925

c. 1925

Raising registered cattle—such as Herefords, Angus, and Beefmasters—has been a major interest of Coloradans since the 1890s, when bulls were imported from Scotland and England to improve the quality of the longhorns from Texas. In the 1940s, Dan Thornton, later Governor Thornton, set a record by selling two bulls for $50,000.

The Sanitary Milking Machine used by The Lewis Dairy Company, Denver.

c. 1905

3—"Jolly Johanna," World's Fair Prize Cow, at Colorado Agricultural College.

c. 1905

702. Feeding Pulp to Cattle at Sugar Plant, Rocky Ford, Colorado

c. 1905

STOCKYARDS, DENVER, COLORADO.

c. 1920

c. 1918

Swift & Company—Prize Draft Team

National Western Stock Show, Denver, Colorado
January 19-26, 1918

c. 1940